SOLILOQUISMS

Other books by the same Author

Novels:

The Vision of Second Samuel

Second Samuel's Vision Revealed

Perry Normel Fun With Liu Syd Dreaming

Winning by Way of Losing

The Quote-A-Thon

SOLILOQUISMS

by Bill Mc Neice

This is a work of original poetry. Any similarity to the published works of other writers is purely coincidental.

Soliloquisms

ISBN: 978 – 1 – 257 – 95693 – 7

Dedication

I have chosen to dedicate the works herein contained to Mrs. Mowhatt, my ninth grade English teacher, and to Mrs. Jean Cohen, my twelfth grade English teacher. These two fine ladies, while not improving my ability to write, used their God-given gifts of love and appreciation to instill in their unskilled and uncaring students a sense of joy in fine literature.

This was not done through the traditional methods of forcing the student to learn what the student will not willingly learn; but rather, through sharing with their students the deep, passionate, ongoing love affair that they have with the great writings of all time. It was in the ecstasy of this sharing that I found awakened within me the appreciation of great works of art and the desire to produce such works myself.

Though I have not, by any stretch of the imagination, even taken the smallest of first steps towards satisfying my desire, I have come to be eternally grateful for the overwhelming privilege of having known these two great ladies. It is because of them that these ragged lines of doggerel are even possible.

Acknowledgments

I would like to gratefully acknowledge and thank from the bottom of my heart my good friend Bill Kaffenberger, founder and head of Loving Kindness Music Co., for granting me permission to reprint the lyrics of three of our songs entitled "LORD, HOW I LOVE YOU", "ACCORDING TO HIS PLAN", and "I SHALL RISE AGAIN".

It should be noted that, although I originally wrote the lyrics to each of these three songs and Bill originally composed and arranged the musical score to each of these three songs, Loving Kindness Music Co. is the sole owner of these three songs, their lyrics, and their musical scores and retains the exclusive rights, including International Copyright, to these songs and any and all use there of. The lyrics of these three songs are reprinted here by permission, granted in writing, of Loving Kindness Music Co., BMI. All rights are reserved.

I would also like to acknowledge and thank Mrs. Katherine M. De Witt, Jr., editor-in-chief of Metropolitan Washington Mensa's monthly newsletter "CAPITAL 'M' ", for using the two poems entitled "THE CAD" and "THE PRINCESS". I consider it a great honor to have two of my poems associated with such a fine periodical as "CAPITAL 'M' ".

Table of Contents

Preface to the Second Edition

This is actually the second edition of this book of poetry. The first was distributed to various people beginning with copies back in 1983. The initial copies of that first edition were done using a very rudimentary text editor and a big, clunky, limited capability line printer.

Since that time, the capabilities of what can be done by a "poet wannabe" have improved tremendously. When the services of multi-versatile web sites such as "Lulu.com" are taken into account, the possibilities become mindless. Irregardless of the literary notoriety of a given person, he can publish his works for others to enjoy. However, it is up to that person to deal with the various indiscrepancies that occur in the writing, editing, and formatting of his works. This second edition is a prime example of such an endeavor.

The obvious difference between this and the first release of this material is in the formatting. Each piece is neatly formatted with headings, page numbering, and highlighted acrostics along with a table of contents to assist in going directly to a particular piece.

There is, as well, the inclusion of variations, omitted from the first edition, to a number of the pieces. These variations may be as simple as a slight change to one or two words within the piece, or as complex as the major rewording of entire stanzas.

Preface continued

In a number of the variations, the differences stem from the author being unable to decide which wording is best for a particular line. In other variations, the author could not decide whether to write the piece as though talking directly to the person to whom the piece refers, or as though talking to others about that person. Rather than making simple choices, the author simply did things both ways and labeled the pieces as variations on a theme.

Probably the biggest difference between the two editions is the assigning of an Opus Number to each piece that can be used to distinguish that individual piece from all of the other pieces ever written by the author. Even if the author, for reasons known only to him, should choose to use the same title for more than one piece, the Opus Number of each piece will easily distinguish between them. This helps tremendously in being able to uniquely identify all of the pieces because the vast majority happen to be untitled.

Along with all of the other changes, the author has managed to deal with a plethora of typos, misspellings, punctuation errors, and the like. While this edition is by no means perfect, it is certainly better in several ways than the first edition. The basic content is essentially identical but the presentation of that content is much MUCH better.

Introduction

There are times when, for reasons totally beyond the comprehension of mere man, half of the sky is filled with a very fine misty rain while in the other half of the sky the golden radiance of the sun reigns supreme over all. It is in times like these that one can see a magnificent band of a multitude of colors stretching from horizon to horizon. This band of colors, known as a rainbow, is formed by the golden sunlight being passed through millions of tiny drops of water in the sky.

In a similar way, each and every person is made up of millions of millions of aspects which form their individual personalities in the person's life. Just as a rainbow stretching from horizon to horizon can not be formed by one solitary drop of water, neither can a person's life be formed by only one or two aspects in that person's personality. Rather, all of the millions of millions of aspects must be taken into account to form a proper understanding of the person.

For this reason it is important to remember that each work herein contained is but one minuscule glimpse of life passed through one single, solitary, and, by itself, insignificant aspect of the millions of millions of aspects that make up the personality. It would be a lie to claim that these works do not give a much more intimate look into their author. But, for the same reason, it would be absurd to try to base a thorough understanding of the author on just the glimpses contained in these works. These works form nothing more and nothing less than a faint glimmer in the dazzling glow of the one who wrote them. It is hoped that this glimmer will be enough to give a rest to those who take the time to bask here.

Opus: 19690000 Nbr: 1 (Laurie)

Untitled Miscellaneous Acrostic

Listen to the falling rain
As it patters out your life
Under winter's wicked strain
Rising up in evil strife.
Insidious little pelter
Enslaving man to shelter.

Opus: 19690000 Nbr: 2 (I love Sally)

Untitled Miscellaneous Acrostic

Insufferable puns fill the stale air

A**l**luding to humor as cuts slice bare.
Sl**o**wly oscillating bodies seek fun.
Abo**v**e, with the sadness of a death begun,
Wing**e**d words slide past with idle bantering,

Twist**s** on a twister mat, and ping-pong tabling
Around **a** Ouija board psychic entranced
With lul**l**ed mind blown on music enhanced
By a large **l**oudness eating at the ears.
At the part**y** melancholy joins tears.

Opus: 19690000 Nbr: 3 (Karen Saginor)

Untitled Miscellaneous Acrostic

Knightly splendor fills the room
Arranged in pseudo happiness.
Remnants of forgotten humor zoom,
Embracing all in a kiss of cloudiness.
Never the less humor is there

Singing softly in the night,
As seen by smiles in the air
Gaily flitting out of sight.
It hides in hearts filled with joy,
Never breaching a sadder hall.
Of all the feelings in the toy,
Rising laughter fills the doll.

Opus: 19690000 Nbr: 4 (Karen)

Untitled Miscellaneous Acrostic

Keepsakes in my mind
Arrange in utter loveliness,
Resembling a kind
Embodiment of her Highness
Never to be left behind.

Opus: 19690000 Nbr: 5

Untitled Miscellaneous

Black cobras curl against the cotton candy clouds,
Rising up from their scarlet nests
        spreading in the city.
Armchair generals win the war at home
While their soldiers die. What a pity.

Gas by the card and food from a ticket,
As nearly all goes to the troops overseas
To stop the eggs across the ocean from laying here.
They drop from vultures of various degrees,

And land and hatch with a deafening roar.
Sirens blare as the snakes soon grow,
Marking desecration of the capitol of the land.
For death creeps o'er the glistening snow.

Opus: 19690000 Nbr: 6 (Dawn)

Untitled Miscellaneous Acrostic

Day is just arriving after night.
A ray of light glistens in the sky
While feathered troubadours sing in flight,
Noticing a lovely Dawn on high.

Opus: 19690000 Nbr: 7

Untitled Miscellaneous

The insect lies in his abode
Deep within the protecting gash.
It was formed many years before.
It arose when the stab of lovelessness
Shook his walk on life's road.
He immediately filled it with trash
To occupy the mind of the growing boor.
Trivial scum was met with needy caress.

Sweet fragrances of joy's perfume
Waft in to tantalize the empty heart.
With the slow creep towards the light
Foolishness, inexperience, and insecurity grow.
Quailing mind blinks in the darkened room
While he hesitates to depart.
Comfort skips across the fleeting night
To happiness he might never know.

Opus: 19690900 Nbr: 1 (Joy Stanley)

Untitled Miscellaneous Acrostic

Joy. A three letter name of happiness.
Only for some the happiness is lost
Yearning for companions. What a mess.

Searching out friends no matter what the cost,
To try and get gladness from their presence.
Anguish comes, leaving fond memories
Next to reality in my essence.
Left are my memories, just like stories
Eating at sanity every moment.
You are my only merriment.

Opus: 19700000   Nbr: 1

Untitled Open Form

In the vast wasteland of sensed information,
O'er the hills of knowledge,
Through the ravines of trivia,
Across the plains of awareness
Comes the enemy force.

Its movement is swift and sure
As it raises great billowing illusions
Before it to hide its approach.
Illusions that cover the earth,
Changing it to a nether world
        of shadow and dream.

Slithering shadows conceal the nagging doubts.
They take many forms, of course, like spies
Sabotaging with a little word or glance,
Creating uncertainty in friendly ranks.
Nothing noticeable, but it's there.

Opus: 19710000 Nbr: 2

Untitled Miscellaneous

A gray shroud covers the sky.
It lies like a rug, thrown over a hole,
Stretched from edge to edge,
With wrinkles going awry
Across its vast sandy soul.
Gray sand lifted from a dredge.

A beautiful shroud, with mounds
Of darkening mist, and caves
In lovely, dark, little shadows.
The weight must be several pounds,
And difficult to hold, for waves
Run by with sharp, aching blows.

But lovely it is, all shiny and bright.
Gunmetal gray and sandy rough,
With its little pinnacles hanging down
Like pins that prick at night.
Given to us off the cuff,
Of course. What a stupid little clown.

I like it, though. I must.
For how could one hate such a wall
With its pimples of light and dark.
Surely hiding the sun is just
To each and every one of us all.
Who could be happy on a day so stark?

Opus: 19710000 Nbr: 1 (Hazel)

Untitled Miscellaneous Acrostic

Happiness is a strange little word
W**a**ndering through the mind of man.
It **z**ips around in a chosen few,
Nev**e**r showing where it once ran.
Lost **l**ong ago, yet still it calls.

Opus: 19710000   Nbr: 3

Untitled Open Form

O'er the hills of knowledge I've climbed,
Through the ravines of trivia,
        often lost and wandering.
Across the plains of awareness?
Perhaps, for I have traveled far.

Always on the banks of Memory,
From the eternal spring of Now
All the way to the Deep Past,
On whose scarred shores I now walk ... alone.

Opus: 19740000 Nbr: 1 (JESUS Lives)

Untitled Miscellaneous Acrostic

Just as morning dawns, bright and fair,
Entering in on a dark dead night,
Slowly revealing all that's there
Under the shadow of our sight,
So some say life is like today.

Lonely little hours disappear
In some quiet meditations,
Visiting The FRIEND, always near,
Enjoying HIS Revelations,
So sure that HE is here to stay.

Opus: 19770114 Nbr: 1 (Becky Rea)

Untitled Miscellaneous Acrostic

Beautiful I cannot use,
Except for starting in this way.
'**C**ause there is something it will lose,
Kind, though, as it is to say.
Yet more, much more, than beauty clear

Rides within her features fine,
Engulfing me with visions dear
As I leave for her this sign.

LORD, How I love YOU (Becky Rea)

Opus: 19770419 Nbr: 1 Lyrics Acrostic

Behold, I walk in this old world.
I wander where I will.
Even though I wander far,
HIS love is with me still.
Caring for me all the day,
HE watches o'er my trail,
Keeping me away from harm
with love that will not fail.

JESUS, LORD, how I love YOU.
YOU've done so much for me.
YOU paid the price for Heaven
when YOU died upon that tree.
JESUS, LORD, how I love YOU.
YOU died to set men free.
YOU opened up old Heaven
when YOU hung upon that tree.
LORD, How I love YOU.

Yes, even though the way is dark
and cold and hard and long,

Rejoicing in HIM all the day,
I cannot suffer wrong.
Eventually my trail will end,
and I will walk no more
As I enter as HIS friend
through Heaven's open door.

JESUS, LORD, how I love YOU.
YOU've done so much for me.
YOU paid the price for Heaven
when YOU died upon that tree.
JESUS, LORD, how I love YOU.
YOU died to set men free.
YOU opened up old Heaven
when YOU hung upon that tree.
LORD, How I love YOU.

Opus: 19770417 Nbr: 1 (Becky Rea)

Untitled Lyrics Acrostic

Between the heartaches and the happies
lies a gulf of unknown sighs,
Entered through a heart that's lonely,
left only if one wins a prize,
Crossed with many doubts and worries
tossed about like fallen leaves.
Kind of hard to see tomorrow,
and yesterday is but a breeze.
Yes, and now I'm doomed to wander
through this empty gulf of mine,

Reaching out into the sadness,
forgetting all the joy behind.
Eventually I'll be a winner
feeling happy all day long.
As for now? ... I'm just a loser
wondering what I'm doing wrong.

Opus: 19770422 Nbr: 1 (Becky Rea)

Untitled Miscellaneous Acrostic

Beside the prose that men write,
Elegant and concise,
Crazy people find delight
Kindling verse for a price.
Yearning to write a crooked rhyme

Revealing some great secret,
Enter they throughout each line
A note without regret.

Opus: 19770422 Nbr: 2 (I love you)

Untitled Miscellaneous Acrostic

I've sent this for you to read

Lest your eyes get lazy.
Or maybe in your hour of need
Vision is growing hazy.
Either way, it comes to you.

Yes, even with my name.
Otherwise it wouldn't do
Unless another took the blame.

Opus: 19770426   Nbr: 1   (Diana Woolls)

Untitled Miscellaneous Acrostic

Day is going, leaving no trace of its flight,
Inflicting on us a great black shroud.
And men bed down in the oncoming night,
Not knowing I am leaving the crowd,
And sitting to think, or perhaps, to write.

What I think doesn't matter.
Only letters interest me.
Organized in endless clatter,
Linked by some strange harmony,
Letters form a worthless chatter
Sailing on an empty sea.

Opus: 19770426 Nbr: 2 (Diana Woolls)

Untitled Miscellaneous Acrostic

During a quiet moment of time,
In a nearly empty room,
A name was placed within my mind,
Neatly to assume
A length difficult to rhyme.

Wouldst that her name
Only had one more letter,
Or one less would do the same.
Leastwise either would be better.
Length, however, is already set.
So I must settle for what I get.

Opus: 19771002 Nbr: 1 (For Diana)

Untitled Miscellaneous Acrostic

Fast the time has come for parting.
    For now it's time to say goodbye.
Over just as it was starting.
    Over faster than a sigh.
Remember I the day it started.
    Remember I the time so well.

Delightful joy to me imparted
    Dainty visions hard to tell.
Inside of me the sorrow's growing
    In this lonely heart of mine
As I know that you are going,
    And we're parted for all time.
Now I've almost finished sharing
    Notes on feelings for today,
And I know I won't stop caring
    As I remind you in this way.

Opus: 19770912 Nbr: 1 (Becky loves Bill's rhyme)

Untitled Miscellaneous Acrostic

By the time my pen runs dry
Each word will be done.
Creating lines that seem to sigh,
Kindled just for fun,
Yet causing thoughts to fly.

Lots of letters do I write,
Or so it seems to me.
Vast hordes that always take delight
Escaping to the sea
Swiftly in the night.

Born of thought, they swim along
Inside my empty head,
Linked together as a throng,
Lost as each word is said
Softly as a song.

Rendered now in black and white,
Hung on the page to dry,
Yet, still there is a trace of fight
Mingled with the sigh
Ensnared in what I write.

Opus: 19771205 Nbr: 1 (Mary is Lovely)

Untitled Lyrics Acrostic

Many memories drift through the idle mind,
C**a**using one to wonder at reality.
Fo**r** the way they come to me is so unkind.
The**y** lack any individuality.

Melt**i**ng fact with fiction in my tired head,
Sight**s** do come and go and merge before my eyes,

Leaving me with much to ponder on my bed.
F**o**r I see the truth and also see the lies.
Li**v**ing such a life is heavy on my heart
As I **e**ndlessly confuse the two I see.
But a **l**ittle joy, at times, it does impart
As I sp**y** the wondrous beauty dreamt in thee.

Opus: 19771211 Nbr: 1 (Mary is Lovely)

Untitled Miscellaneous Acrostic

My my, I am so unconfused
As I think of you this day,
Revealing how I've used
Your name in such a way.

Implanting in each line one letter
Straight along one edge,

Locked within this clumsy fetter
Of words used as a hedge.
Vexing some with idle chatter,
Even for so short a time,
Leaving notes within the clatter,
Your name within the rhyme.

Opus: 19771218 Nbr: 1 (Mary Dream For Me)

Untitled Miscellaneous Acrostic

Mediocrity, oozing down the page
without a thing to say
As I sit and think of words to use
in writing a stupid rhyme,
Reveals what a narrow little life
I've led until today.
Yet, I have no right to think that
things are changing with passing time.

During the previous years
I have experienced much to tell,
Remembered as fleeting glances in the wee
small hours of the night.
Even though they are deep within me,
I cannot find where they dwell,
And even if I could, words would not express
feelings brought to light.
My narrow mind will not respond
to what has happened in my life.

For I don't see the key to stringing words
together in a row,
Organized in little lines, telling tales
of victory from strife.
Rather, I sit and waste my time
trying to feel what I can't know,

Missing from my heart abilities to dream
a dream of real life.
Even so, I ask for the dreams of one
to lead me as I go.

Opus: 19771212 Nbr: 1 (Mikki)

Untitled Miscellaneous Acrostic

Minor little memories grow within my mind
Inflicting moments of pleasure on my head.
Knightly splendor breaks apart,
        allowing me to find
Keepsakes of pure joy to treasure up instead.
In my heart a name I cannot leave behind.

Opus: 19780218 Nbr: 1 (Libby Whitt)

Untitled Miscellaneous Acrostic

Little flakes of virgin snow,
In hidden fits of great delight,
Barely see the sun aglow
Before they melt right out of sight,
Yearning for its warmth to know.

What causes things to be this way
Hardly seems to matter much
In times when you are here to stay.
Troubled, though, am I by such
The moment that you go away.

Opus: 19790120 Nbr: 1 (Mary Kathleen)

Untitled Lyrics Acrostic

Memories sustain me now,
As I go along my way,
Recalling all the times I've been
Yearning for her to stay.

Kind of hard to clear my mind
And think of some other things.
There's one joy I'd like to find,
Happiness her love brings.
Living now is so unreal,
Engulfed in dreams that I see.
Even though they are not so,
Nicer are dreams to me.

Opus: 19790120 Nbr: 1 continued

More and more I dream of her,
And it's fun, I must confess,
Recalling all the times I've been
Yearning for her caress.

Kind of like to take her hand
And promise we'd never part,
Then I think I'd understand
Happiness in my heart.
Living now is so unreal,
Engulfed in dreams that I see.
Even though they are not so,
Nicer are dreams to me.

Opus: 19790927 Nbr: 1 (Mary Gruber)

Untitled Miscellaneous Acrostic

Morning slowly tries to come
After many sleepless nights,
Reaching for the lonely one,
Yearning for vain delights.

Gently GOD will strike it dumb.
Ripped with hoe and torn with plow
Underneath the MASTER's hand,
Breaks HE up his fallow ground,
Ending one more selfish plan.
Rests he in his GOD for now.

Many times he went astray,
And he'll probably stray some more,
Roaming from the peaceful bay.
Yet back home he'll come for sure.

GOD won't let him stay away.
Reaching for the wayward one
Underneath HIS mighty hand,
Breaks HE every wall of sin,
Easing grace into the man.
Rests he in his GOD again.

Opus: 19791129 Nbr: 1

Untitled Miscellaneous

The grass slowly withers
'neath the cold harsh wind
As adults and children
quickly hasten to the stores.
No one seems to notice
the slow gentle change along the way.
The sky has turned a deep rich blue,
and the moors

Are now golden brown
in the soft silent sunlight.
But to the stores the people go,
just to turn for home
All laden with packages
and cards to send away.
There's nary a thought of the hills
where children used to roam.

Opus: 19791129 Nbr: 1 continued

The air grows cold and the days short
as we scurry to and fro
All bundled up in our tawdry little tasks,
ignoring the quiet peace
That lies just beyond our grasp.
The empty wooded lots call to us,
And the tiny rivulets sing our names
in every little crease.

But we have learned too much
to hear their voices cry.
We no longer gaze into the sky
or savor the meadows mist.
Instead, we spread our concrete jungles,
and hustle back and forth,
Forgetting their big secret.
Ignorance is bliss.

Opus: 19791207 Nbr: 1

Untitled Miscellaneous

The hustle and bustle of life goes on,
As cars go racing to and fro
On asphalt ribbons tied in knots.
And when they've gone where e'er they go,
The people hurry and scurry out
From cars to buildings, rushing so.
They run at such a frantic pace
To lose what little peace they know.

But as for me, I've run that race.
I've felt the drive to hurry on
And do the same as all the rest.
I lost the beauty of the dawn.
With evening just a jumbled mess,
I wondered where my day had gone.
There wasn't time for anything.
Not even time to stop and yawn.

But then one day I stopped and looked,
And saw the sky a royal blue,
And as I slowed and looked around,
I noticed grass still damp with dew.
The sun was shining in the sky
As overhead some birds still flew
To look for food or maybe rest.
To me it seemed so wholly new.

To stop and sit and gaze across
A field at trees that gently sway
With every bit of breeze or wind,
Or maybe on a sunny day
To take a casual little stroll
Down some forgotten path or way.
It seems too foolish to pursue,
But peace it brings to those who stay.

Opus: 19791211   Nbr: 1   (Laurie)

Untitled Miscellaneous Acrostic

Let me sit and think of you as days go by,
And recall the little sparkle in your eye,
Undimmed by ages past or years to come.
Realize your smile shines just like the sun
In the tiny quiet chambers of my mind
Enticing me to write. For you are so kind.

Opus: 19791213 Nbr: 1 (Laurie)

Untitled Lyrics Acrostic

Look and see the sunshine pouring from her smile,
And just watch the little twinkle in her eyes.
Understand her laughter, gently for a while
Resting on a cloud beneath the skies.
In the quiet of the day
    she will come and walk my way.
Enjoying what we have to say,
    I wish that she could stay.

According to HIS Plan

Opus: 19791218 Nbr: 1 Lyrics

Listen to the gentle call
    of ripples on the lake
    as they slowly wash across the shore.
Listen to the whispers
    of the wind among the trees
    telling of the ONE whom they adore.

    HE's the ONE who made the patterns
        that we see upon the sand.
    HE holds the trees within HIS mighty hand.
    I don't know the future
        nor does any other man,
    But the future goes according to HIS Plan.

Listen to the quiet song
of stars up in the sky
softly singing of HIS majesty.
Listen to the little birds
as they begin to fly
calling for HIS coming, soon to be.

HE's the ONE who made the patterns
that we see upon the sand.
HE holds the trees within HIS mighty hand.
I don't know the future
nor does any other man,
But the future goes according to HIS Plan.

Listen to HIS Prophets
as they share HIS Holy Word
telling what HE says is gonna be.
Listen as HE tells us
of HIS love for all mankind,
how HE died so HE could set us free.

HE's the ONE who made the patterns
that we see upon the sand.
HE holds the trees within HIS mighty hand.
I don't know the future
nor does any other man,
But the future goes according to HIS Plan.

Listen to the triumph
of that Resurrection Day
proving HIM to be Almighty GOD.
Let us come and join the wind,
the ripples, and the stars
giving HIM the Glory and the Laud.

HE's the ONE who made the patterns
that we see upon the sand.
HE holds the trees within HIS mighty hand.
I don't know the future
nor does any other man,
But the future goes according to HIS Plan.

Opus: 19791118 Nbr: 1

Untitled Miscellaneous

Apples make a tasty sauce,
And a peach goes well with cream,
But as for us, we're not the same,
Or so to me it seems.

Yet, there's a gift you have from me.
You've had it from the start.
For you're the only one, you see,
Who will always have my heart.

For though you've lost this shadow,
And I'm not near you all the while,
My cloudy days still shine with joy
In the sunlight of your smile.

For, knowing what your smiles do,
If you should choose to frown at me,
Smiles still are coming through,
Living in my memory.

The Cad (Alice)

Opus: 19810703 Nbr: 1 Miscellaneous Acrostic

Across the endless deserts
that form the sands of time,
Lots of winding paths are left
by each and every man.
In every path are left the marks
of a story line
Created by the footprints
across the shifting sands.
Even I have left my prints.
The marks of the heel are mine.

I Shall Rise Again (JESUS)

Opus: 19800412 Nbr: 1 Lyrics Acrostic

Judgments swiftly sweep across
the giant human sea,
and come to rest on ME
as I die to set men free.

Everything I've said and done
has led up to this day.
For it's the only way
they could ever hope to pay.

Oh, to live,
and walk with them that second mile.
To live in them,
and see them smile.

Sadly now I bear the pain
of Hell for all mankind.
They asked ME for a sign,
and this is all they'll find.
Up upon a rugged cross
I die to set them free,
and give them victory,
if they'll only trust in ME.

Oh, to live,
and walk with them that second mile.
To live in them,
and see them smile.

Sadly now I give MY life
to pay for all their sin,
but this is not the end.
For I shall rise again.

Tetelestai! ... It is finished! ...
Their debt ... is at ... an end.

Opus: 19800826 Nbr: 1 (Laurel Mc Cain)

Untitled Lyrics Acrostic

Looking out across a clear blue sky
All I see are clouds adrifting by
Until I'm with her.
Reminders of all the times we've had
Enter in my mind and they make me glad,
Longing to be with her.

More and more I think of her
as I pass on through the night,
Choosing words to write for her
that I hope will turn out right

'**C**ause I want to be with her.
All I do is think of her
as the days go passing by.
In my quiet memories
I can almost hear her sigh.
Now I want to be with her.

Let me think of her as the days go by,
And recall the sparkle of her eye,
Until I'm with her.
Reaching out to things I've just begun
Everything just seems to come undone,
Longing to be with her.

More and more I think of her
as I pass on through the night,
Choosing words to write for her
that I hope will turn out right

'**C**ause I want to be with her.
All I do is think of her
as the days go passing by.
In my quiet memories
I can almost hear her sigh.
Now I want to be with her.

Opus: 19800914 Nbr: 1 (Mary, Jean)

Untitled Lyrics Acrostic

Mixed emotions are all I have for you,
And I can't decide exactly what to do.
Reaching out to find you in the lonely night,
Yet, I don't want to see you in the broad daylight.

Just a thought I had o'er a year ago,
Everything just seemed to be a working out so,
And then you seemed just to turn away.
Now I can't decide if I should go or stay.

Many memories drift through my tired mind,
And reality just seems to fall behind.
Remembering both the good and the bad,
Yearning for your happiness I make you sad.

Journeying through this tangled web
Everything is flowing at a low low ebb.
All this confusion is a driving me mad.
Now I'm glad I met you ... Now I wish I never had.

Opus: 19801026 Nbr: 1 (Debbie Hallet)

Untitled Lyrics Acrostic

Distant memories
    from some halfway forgotten dreams
Enter in and sweep across my mind.
By the time I get to see them,
    they've up and gone away
Back to a place impossible to find.

Dream, let me dream on.
Let reality keep slipping 'round the bend.
Dream, let me dream on.
Oh, I hope this dream won't ever have to end.

In the quiet of my memories,
    in the shelter of my mind,
Every day I walk a little while

Hoping that I'll see her,
and be with her again,
And perhaps I'll even see her smile.

Dream, let me dream on.
Let reality keep slipping 'round the bend.
Dream, let me dream on.
Oh, I hope this dream won't ever have to end.

Listening to these gentle thoughts
as they drift on through my mind,
Lots of things just seem to fade away.
Every time I dream of her
I hope it will never end,
Though reality grows fainter every day.

Dream, let me dream on.
Let reality keep slipping 'round the bend.
Dream, let me dream on.
Oh, I hope this dream won't ever have to end.

Opus: 19801206 Nbr: 1

Untitled Lyrics

In the quiet of the morning
while the dew lies on the grass,
The sun slowly rises,
and the stars start fading fast.
The morning mist quickly melts away
from its place among the trees,
And life flows gently like a breeze.

LORD, I tend to hurry.
LORD, I tend to worry.
Accept my thank you, please,
For making me flow gently like a breeze.

In the quiet of the evening
at the setting of the sun,
The birds have hushed their singing,
and the crickets just begun.
The moon slowly rises
from back behind the trees,
And life flows gently like a breeze.

LORD, I tend to hurry.
LORD, I tend to worry.
Accept my thank you, please,
For making me flow gently like a breeze.

Opus: 19801206 Nbr: 1 continued

When I see a problem coming,
        or I feel anxiety,
When the pressures start to build up
        and come to rest on me,
I wish I'd learn to come to YOU
        down upon my knees,
Then I'd flow gently like the breeze.

        LORD, I tend to hurry.
        LORD, I tend to worry.
        Accept my thank you, please,
        For making me flow gently like a breeze.

Opus: 19810123 Nbr: 1 (Deby)

Untitled Lyrics Acrostic

Down the quiet corridors
that wind all through my mind
I wander all the time
hoping that I'll find
Even just a glimpse of her
where I may sit and stay.
For it's a pleasant way
to brighten up my day.

Oh, I'd love
to be alone with her a while,
To hear her laugh,
and see her smile.

By the time I catch my glimpse,
it's up and gone away
to wait another day
before it comes to stay.

Yet I know it's for the best
for her to be so free.
So I wait patiently,
hoping she'll find me.

Oh, I'd love
to be alone with her a while,
To hear her laugh,
and see her smile.

Opus: 19810417 Nbr: 1 (Deby)

Untitled Lyrics Acrostic

Down the quiet corridors of my mind
I find myself a wandering all the time
hoping I'll catch a glimpse,
where I may sit and stay,
of the one that I love before she goes away.
Even though I fear she can't be mine,
I find I'm dreaming of her all the time
hoping there'll come a day
when I can clearly see
a glimmer of love within her heart for me.

Oh, I know I should stop dreaming,
but my dreams will never end
until I learn to cope with what is real.

Oh, I know I should stop dreaming,
but dreams are all I have
to help me get along with how I feel.

Before she came along my life was fine.
I was almost feeling happy part of the time,
then she entered in my world
and took a major part,
and now she's the one that occupies my heart.
Yesterday my life was going fine.
Today I'm dreaming of her all the time.
Tomorrow ... I live in fear
that she must go away.
So I run to my dreams to find a better day.

Oh, I know I should stop dreaming,
but my dreams will never end
until I learn to cope with what is real.

Oh, I know I should stop dreaming,
but dreams are all I have
to help me get along with how I feel.

Opus: 19810521 Nbr: 1 Var: 1

Untitled Lyrics

I use to like to walk within the cities,
Listening to the roaring of the crowd,
But now I hear the whispers of the mountains
Floating past my ears upon a cloud.

> I wish that I could walk upon the mountains.
> I wish I could roam among the hills.
> The days out in the country seem so peaceful,
> Better than the cities and their thrills.

The night is gently rolled back like a curtain,
As a bright and clear day comes along.
The sunlight softly settles on the mountains,
And I see the darkness has all gone.

> I wish that I could walk upon the mountains.
> I wish I could roam among the hills.
> The days out in the country seem so peaceful,
> Better than the cities and their thrills.

Opus: 19810521 Nbr:1 Var: 1 continued

The morning mist quickly melts out of the hollows
As the birds begin to sing and fly.
The morning softly melts into the evening
As another day goes passing by.

> I wish that I could walk upon the mountains.
> I wish I could roam among the hills.
> The days out in the country seem so peaceful,
> Better than the cities and their thrills.

The evening slowly drifts across the ridges,
And the stars shine brightly in the night.
The crickets sweetly sing out to each other,
And one feels the world will turn out right.

> I wish that I could walk upon the mountains.
> I wish I could roam among the hills.
> The days out in the country seem so peaceful,
> Better than the cities and their thrills.

Opus: 19810521 Nbr: 1 Var: 2

Untitled Lyrics

I use to like to walk within the cities,
Listening to the roaring of the crowd,
But now I hear the whispers of the mountains
Floating past my ears upon a cloud.

I wish that I could walk upon the mountains.
I wish I could roam among the hills.
The days out in the country seem so peaceful,
Better than the cities and their thrills.

The rain is gently drawn back like a curtain,
As a bright and clear day comes along.
The sunlight softly settles on the mountains,
And I see the dark clouds have all gone.

I wish that I could walk upon the mountains.
I wish I could roam among the hills.
The days out in the country seem so peaceful,
Better than the cities and their thrills.

Opus: 19810521 Nbr: 1 Var: 2 continued

The raccoons stop their playing with each other
Just so they can start to play some more.
The meadow mouse so quickly runs for cover
As one walks across the valley floor.

I wish that I could walk upon the mountains.
I wish I could roam among the hills.
The days out in the country seem so peaceful,
Better than the cities and their thrills.

The evening slowly drifts across the ridges,
And the stars shine brightly in the night.
The crickets sweetly sing out to each other,
And one feels the world will turn out right.

I wish that I could walk upon the mountains.
I wish I could roam among the hills.
The days out in the country seem so peaceful,
Better than the cities and their thrills.

Opus: 19810710   Nbr: 1   (Sonia)

Untitled Miscellaneous Acrostic

Silently I sit and dream
Over growing spans of time,
Noticing a lovely queen
In the shadows of my mind;
And I know it's you I've seen.

Opus: 19810714   Nbr: 1   (Alice)

Untitled Miscellaneous Acrostic

After day is gone from sight,
Lost within the office grind,
I am left to find delight
Chasing angels through my mind,
Even you through out the night.

Opus: 19810804 Nbr: 1 (Sonia Hernandez)

Untitled Shakespearian Sonnet Acrostic

So quietly the evening comes to light
On all the frets and worries of the day.
Now all beneath the silent shroud of night
Is laid to rest as troubles fade away.
A princess gleaming in the dark I see,

Held fast within my tangled web of dream
Extending far beyond what e'er can be.
Rare diamonds, though they glitter brightly, seem
No match compared to sparkles in her eyes.
A voice she has that nothing can come near.
Next to her skin are silks but ragged lies.
Delighted by the glow of one so dear,
Ecstatic praise I cast beneath her feet
Zipped out upon this tawdry paper sheet.

Opus: 19811010 Nbr: 1 (Alice)

Untitled Lyrics Acrostic

Across the endless deserts
that form the sands of time
Lots of winding paths are left
by each and every man.
In each path his character
is written line by line,
Created by the footprints
he has left behind.
Even I had left my prints.
The marks of the heel were mine.

As I looked, no meaning
or purpose could I find
Locked within the footprints
I had left behind.
I'd only wandered aimlessly
across the burning sand.
Causing lots of problems
for every other man.
Even I had left my prints.
The marks of the heel were mine.

As I gazed across the sand
        toward the end of my lifetime
Looking for some meaning
        or purpose I could find
I saw a set of footprints
        with purpose crossing mine.
CHRIST's footprints have a purpose
        for each and every man.
Even I could change my prints.
        Some marks to be healed were mine.

As I travel on across
        the endless sands of time,
Looking to CHRIST's footprints
        as my guiding line,
I find I have a purpose
        within HIS Master Plan,
Caring for the others
        lost in the burning sand.
Even I have changed my prints.
        The marks that were healed are mine.

Opus: 19811105 Nbr: 1 (Debi)

Untitled Miscellaneous Acrostic

Down the road a little ways
 is a Hallmark store
Entered very easily
 through its double door,
But no card like this you'll find
 if you look in there.
It is written just for you
 'cause you are so rare.

Opus: 19811107 Nbr: 1 (Alice)

Untitled Miscellaneous Acrostic

As I sit here for a time
Looking for something to say,
I see a figure with loveliness sublime
Carefully reading on this day,
Enjoying, I hope, this rhyme.

Opus: 19811112 Nbr: 1 (Mary Jean Gruber)

Untitled Petrarchan Sonnet Acrostic

Misquoted moodiness may often seem
An indecisiveness within my mind
Retained in place of joy I could not find.
Yet, others taste the richness of its cream.

Joy always seemed elusive like a dream
Extending far beyond my gloomy mind.
Alas, I feared I just could not unwind,
Nor could I be a member of its team.

Go far from me you melancholy swine.
Return from whence your evil sadness came.
Undaunted now, I see a victory.
Beneath this somber moodiness of mine
Extends a joy within my SAVIOUR's Name,
Revealed throughout HIS wondrous love for me.

The Princess (Sarah)

Opus: 19811207 Nbr: 1 Miscellaneous Acrostic

Sunlight softly dances in her eye,
And her lips so gently shape a smile.
Radiant sparkles glow throughout the sky
As I gaze at her for just a while,
Happy as I see her passing by.

Opus: 19811216 Nbr: 1

Untitled Shakespearian Sonnet

Her hair does shine, but not like golden suns.
Her eyes are dark, not glistening like the dew.
Her lips are not the velvet cushioned ones.
Her voice? Like angels? It would never do.

And yet, her hair does shimmer in the light.
Her eyes contain a quiet little glow,
And when she smiles it always comes out right.
To hear her voice is loveliness to know.

For though her features speak of beauty clear,
It's not the type that one can plainly see.
For it's the beauty that one holds so dear,
The kind that comes from love and purity.

And as she ages it will not depart.
For it is JESUS living in her heart.

The Angel (Cassandra)

Opus: 19811218 Nbr: 1 Miscellaneous Acrostic

Could angels take the form of man
And walk within our world,
So surely would I know their plan
So silently unfurled.
As quietly they mixed right in,
Not noticed at the start,
Down o'er the ages they'd begin
Revealing to our heart
A beauty like she has within.

Opus: 19811219 Nbr: 1 (Cassandra)

Untitled Lyrics Acrostic

Crystalline cathedrals
with their walls so bright,
Amber lights and signals
flashing through the night,
Silver spoons and platters
polished up just right
Shine not by comparison
to her quiet light.
Angels with their halos
all polished and aglow
Next to her are nothing
but coal dust on the snow.
Diamonds and emeralds
just refuse to show
Radiance and glitter
within her gentle glow.
And within her features fair,
a beauty past compare.

Opus: 19811231 Nbr: 1 (Philomena Abeyta)

Untitled Petrarchan Sonnet Acrostic

Perhaps, if all eternity were time
Held fast within my tiny little mind,
In all its vastness maybe I could find
Loquacious words to write of her in rhyme.
Or if I had the talent of a mime,
Mere gestures I could use of such a kind
Expressing all the joy she leaves behind.
Near ecstasy she makes my feelings climb.
Aah so, the struggle must continue on
Between my feelings and the words I know.
Ensnared am I on joy I cannot show.
Yet still, I scribble on from dusk to dawn
To try to find a way to show upon
A rhyme the happiness within her glow.

Opus: 19820000 Nbr: 1

Untitled Miscellaneous

The flowers gently quiver in the breeze.
The sunlight softly settles on the trees.
I feel a hushed excitement coming on,
Just sitting here and watching a new dawn.

The day will drift along by passing hours.
Some butterflies may stop and kiss some flowers.
The morning light will slowly fade away
As evening comes to mark the end of day.

Opus: 19820206 Nbr: 1 (Sarah Cassandra)

Untitled Shakespearian Sonnet Acrostic

So rapidly the tiny moments fly
As I, awake within a wondrous dream,
Recall, in gentle whispers of a sigh,
A beauty far beyond what e'er can seem
Held fast within my tiny little heart.

Could I find words of loveliness divine,
And to such words a vibrant life impart,
So shoddy are their features next to thine.
Such words to you I never can compare,
And neither can a poet write a rhyme
Nor sonnet showing elegance so rare,
Distilled within a beauty so sublime.
Revealed within the wonder that is you,
A dream I know forever will be true.

Opus: 19820210 Nbr: 1 (Sonia)
Untitled Miscellaneous Acrostic

Someday I'll walk on streets of gold
O'er which the angels trod so free.
Not 'till, I hope, that I grow old.
Instead, an angel now I see.
And so it's you that I behold.

Opus: 19820627 Nbr: 1 (Sarah)
Untitled Miscellaneous Acrostic

So gently silhouetted 'gainst the sky
A pleasant dream goes drifting through my mind,
Remembered in the evenings with a sigh,
And leaving such a happiness behind,
Held fast as I go floating through the sky.

Opus: 19821107 Nbr: 1 (Alice)

Untitled Miscellaneous Acrostic

Alas, a fog I see has drifted by.
Low now it lies upon a murky sea.
In banks of banks it blinds my wistful eye.
Could such a fog just lift and I could see,
E'er more could you be found within my eye.

Opus: 19821120 Nbr: 1 (Sarah Cassandra)

Untitled Petrarchan Sonnet Acrostic

So little time there ever seems to be,
Across the span of years I call my life,
Reminding me of joy above the strife
Around the endless struggle that is me.
How often do I wish that I could see,

Concealed somewhere, a sharp and able knife.
And it could quickly cut away the strife,
So letting all the happiness flow free.
Somehow, I feel I've found just such a knife,
And what a lovely one she seems to be.
Now if for one like me she would employ
Don't-ask-me-what-it-is against my strife,
Removing all the harshness that I see,
A life of peace I think I could enjoy.

Opus: 19821127   Nbr: 1   (Sonia)
Untitled Miscellaneous Acrostic

So quietly the years go quickly by,
Or so it seems to those who count the days.
No matter, though, to one that's such as I.
Instead, I merely count the different ways
A princess holds the heavens in her eye.

Opus: 19821205 Nbr: 1 (Sarah)

Untitled Lyrics Acrostic

Silver throated troubadours
go sailing through the sky,
And the sun arising,
bids the night goodbye,
Reminding me of all HE's done,
And how HE set me free,
Handing out salvation
to a wretch like me.

And I know GOD's SON has risen.
HE brought forth the never ending day.
HE paid the price no one else could pay,
And HE bids us now to follow...HIS way.

Slowly now HE molds my life
as it ought to be,
And HE gives me joy
and peace abundantly.
Removing all the guilt and pain,
And filling me with love,
Hope abounds within my heart
when I seek above.

And I know GOD's SON has risen.
HE brought forth the never ending day.
HE paid the price no one else could pay,
And HE bids us now to follow...HIS way.

Opus: 19830123 Nbr: 1 (Sonia)

Untitled Miscellaneous Acrostic

Should all eternity be mine to see,
O'er all its vastness I could never find
No loveliness to e'er compare to thee
In any way except to be unkind.
Above it all you seem to be to me.

Opus: 19830130 Nbr: 1 (Sarah Cassandra)

Untitled Petrarchan Sonnet Acrostic

Should I but sit and dream as time goes by,
And let my mind but wander through the days
Remembering the things of greatest praise,
A lot of things could pass my wistful eye,
Held fast like clouds against a speckled sky.

Could I but choose the one on which there lays
A glory far exceeding all the praise
Surrounding all the others that I spy?
Suppose I chose the greatest I could find
Among the things of praise that I could see.
Now on its right a place for you there'd be,
Dreamt in the quiet corners of my mind,
Revealing such a choice as purely blind
Against the greater glory found in thee.

Opus: 19830123 Nbr: 2

Untitled Lyrics

So many years ago
    CHRIST walked earth like a man.
When only thirty three
    HE carried out HIS Plan.
HE died upon a cross
    to pay for all our sin,
And give eternal life
    to all who trust in HIM.

Maybe today...
    CHRIST will come again.
JESUS said HE's coming back
    to take us home with HIM.
Maybe today...
    CHRIST will come again.
JESUS said HE's coming back
    but wouldn't tell us when.
Maybe today...

When CHRIST was crucified
some thought it was the end,
Forgetting promises
that HE would rise again.
HE rose up from the dead
to prove HIS victory,
So those who trust in HIM
could live eternally.

Maybe today...
CHRIST will come again.
JESUS said HE's coming back
to take us home with HIM.
Maybe today...
CHRIST will come again.
JESUS said HE's coming back
but wouldn't tell us when.
Maybe today...

For forty days and nights
        from Resurrection Day
HE walked with us some more
        before HE went HIS way.
HE promised to return,
        a thief within the night,
To take along with HIM
        all those whose hearts are right.

Maybe today...
        CHRIST will come again.
JESUS said HE's coming back
        to take us home with HIM.
Maybe today...
        CHRIST will come again.
JESUS said HE's coming back
        but wouldn't tell us when.
Maybe today...

So as I watch and pray
for CHRIST to come again,
I purify my heart
from all the guilt and sin.
For when CHRIST does return,
I want my heart just right.
So I will live each day
like HE'll return that night.

Maybe today...
CHRIST will come again.
JESUS said HE's coming back
to take us home with HIM.
Maybe today...
CHRIST will come again.
JESUS said HE's coming back
but wouldn't tell us when.
Maybe today...

www.ingramcontent.com/pod-product-compliance
Ingram Content Group UK Ltd.
Pitfield, Milton Keynes, MK11 3LW, UK
UKHW041935190726
13854UKWH00004B/1596